# FIELDS AWAY

# SARAH WARDLE

# *FIELDS AWAY*

BLOODAXE BOOKS

ISBN: 1 85224 620 0

First published 2003 by
Bloodaxe Books Ltd,
Highgreen,
Tarset,
Northumberland NE48 1RP.

**www.bloodaxebooks.com**
For further information about Bloodaxe titles
please visit our website or write to
the above address for a catalogue.

Bloodaxe Books Ltd acknowledges
the financial assistance of Arts Council England.

Cover printing by J. Thomson Colour Printers Ltd, Glasgow.

Printed in Great Britain by
Cromwell Press Ltd, Trowbridge, Wiltshire.

*To my parents*
*for bringing me through*

# Acknowledgements

Acknowledgements are due to the editors of the following publications in which some of these poems first appeared: *The Interpreter's House, London Magazine, Metre, PN Review, Poetry Review, Thumbscrew* and *The Times Literary Supplement.*

Fifteen of these poems made up my submission for the Geoffrey Dearmer Prize, *Poetry Review*'s New Poet of the Year Award, which I won in 1999. A selection appeared in *Anvil New Poets 3*, edited by Roddy Lumsden and Hamish Ironside (Anvil, 2001).

I would like to thank Southern and South East Arts and Bedgebury National Pinetum for my residency in summer 2002.

'On Westminster Bridge' was commissioned by Shakespeare's Globe for *'Earth has not any thing to shew more fair'*, edited by Peter Oswald, Alice Oswald and Robert Woof (Shakespeare's Globe and The Wordsworth Trust, 2002).

# Contents

Dear Debbie & Ed,

Sorry I didn't see you during my usual summer holiday — Change. I keep meaning to write to you and then the moment passes — apologies.

Sadie this year I sent you a flyer on my niece Sarah's book and thought you might like a copy.

Best wishes
M

## Arcadia

As if a country kitchen were where we sat
and you wore a smock, and I an apron,
as I rocked a newborn asleep in his cot,
while through the door came laughter from our other children,

and this table, instead of papers and books,
held a jug of ale and a weekly wage,
while the scent of baked ham spread as it cooked,
and with one hand I stirred in onion and sage,

I caught you lift your straggling thoughts over a fence,
your face framed offguard, gazing fields away,
as you herded your words into a sentence,
your eyes brown and deep as the soil's clay.

# Reading Room Requiem

Suppose a poet had been last to leave
the Reading Room, the final cell to die
in the giant brain that enclosed the eye
of its great domed mind, had been first to receive

the impression of the pews of learning
sitting empty, the god of knowledge gone,
fled through a hole, as in the Pantheon,
shelves raided, books stacked as if for burning,

suppose he'd seen all this and then, turning,
had shrugged and walked out beneath the golden orb
of the British Museum, quite absorbed
in imagination with ideas churning,

detached as Nero declaiming a song
of Troy's destruction as Rome blazed,
men torched monuments, temples were razed,
suppose him cold-hearted as he went along,

but picture him warmed by a current of thought,
pausing trivially to feel the heat
from hot chestnut coals in Great Russell Street,
pleased to find an image he had not sought.

# On Westminster Bridge

Pause for a moment on Westminster Bridge,
freeze the Thames, turn passing cars to stone,
suspend the rain, still the speedboat's flag,
stop the Prime Minister in mid-flow,
cast the people in bronze, anchor the barge,
say *Sleep* to a vendor in a hot dog van,
shut the London Eye, let a gull not budge,
remove the battery from Big Ben.
Now hold it there for two hundred years,
the time it would take us to travel upstream
to Wordsworth, and further on to Shakespeare,
or down to the twenty-third century.
Shrink the present into fourteen lines.
Sign your sonnet and post it on the tide.

## Sceptic's Song
*(after Montale)*

I fear one day, as I walk down the street,
I shall see through the window of the world.
Looking over my shoulder, my eyes will meet
a void, no drunk's vision, but a vacant whirl.

Then reality will vanish, the reel turn
and illusion again be projected on
all nothingness, but in me the truth will burn,
for I'll know that I too am part of the con.


## Urban Symphony

*Nought may endure but Mutability.*
The river of rain in the gutter of the city
can't be trodden in twice,
and the woman who steps off the kerb
isn't the same as a minute before.
She has crossed the road, disappeared through a door.

Red, red and amber, green:
watch how the traffic lights
conduct change, while in between
we're trapped in the present tense of a verb,
as cars roll by and people wait,
and pedestrians stand and conjugate

the future till the traffic stops,
when the disparate crowd starts to cross,
all heading their separate ways,
like thoughts disseminating through a maze,
suddenly finding that they've filed
across the street and strolled on half a mile.

# Music for an Empty Ballroom

Come the revolution, when the embers
of a Bechstein burn in Piccadilly
and the bodies of the rich lie six deep,
lining the Mall, when citizens are spilling

out of their estates in Hackney and Brixton,
drinking champagne and digging up the lawn
in the Palace grounds, when Wednesday is Sunday
and a couple are raiding the National Gallery,

carrying off a Bruegel to their new rooms
in Park Lane, when a river of people
is flooding down The Strand and Whitehall,
when revellers with bottles sing *Swing Low*

by Big Ben, when a single mother
sits on the Queen's throne in Parliament,
when teenagers wander off the street
to take their seats in the House, when an Asian girl

stands and speaks at the Despatch Box,
and a black man and woman cradle the Mace
in their arms, when the general who led them
strides down a red carpet, disorientated for a second

in the Palace maze, and a woman who hears him
holds her breath in a locked bathroom,
where she lies on the floor, bruised and left for dead,
let him pass an open door and pause in the hallway,

and imagine he hears in that moment, by a trick
of the mind, music for an empty ballroom
rising to a crescendo, but let him blink
and say to himself, *It is only the wind.*

## On Rereading *King Lear*

*(after Keats)*

Once more King Lear is raging on the heath,
the Fool is duelling with him, crossing words,
Poor Tom acts in a theatre that's absurd,
and reason's on the run from fact and truth,
for language, like an exile, can take flight
from sense, when meanings, like uprooted stems,
are blown away to scatter on the wind
and sow the seeds of rambling fear and doubt.
I know because I once played Lear myself,
and wandered far inside a foreign land,
whose speech and men I couldn't understand,
that winter, dressed in an asylum shift.
Our rights are loaned. In these unsettled times,
fate could turn us out of our homes and minds.

# Laws of Disturbance

If you apply constant pressure,
happiness is proportional to ideas.
Ideas travel at the speed of thought
and differ only in their wavelength.
Wavelength can be ascertained
if you know how soon an answer comes.

Answers are only ever emitted
from dark questions, which absorb passion when heated.
The total current of passion flowing in
must be the same as the passion leaving.
When passion moves faster than the thought it generates,
then mania is set up behind it.

The acuteness of an incidence of mania
depends on the refracted angle in the other media.
If a refracted angle exceeds the critical one,
total internal reflection of the self will happen.
When selves associate to form a pair,
superconductivity of synapses occurs.

As the siren of the synaptic orchestra draws nearer,
frequency of self-importance and pitch grow higher.
Once your importance starts to gather momentum,
it has a tendency to keep on moving.
When you're on a roll, opposing force
is all that'll make your anger cease.

Your anger stops and emotions change direction,
when a change in flux is caused by sedation.
The change in flux is in direct proportion
to the length and severity of depression.
The depressive is one of two colliding spheres:
one's energy picks up; the other's disappears.

Equilibrium can be reached when a mind
is balanced on a knife-edge, or rooted on the ground.
In the subatomic world of mood,
we can measure only intensity, or truth.
If we were to rewind the universe,
joy and grief would reduce to the same force.

# Psyche

Yesterday life was faster and fuller than this,
when I arrived here, barefoot, with clenched fist,
ready to kick and punch. Yes, I fought.
Having travelled the earth to find him, I was distraught,
seeking him who came to me divinely in the night,
always in darkness, invisible, so that it might
all have been a dream, but one I believed.

I journeyed here, hoping to be received
in this, his house, his palace, his temple,
with him at the top of the aisle by the oracle,
extending his hand like a bridegroom. It was a trick.
I tried to escape, ran down corridors, looked for an exit,
like Theseus without Ariadne's thread.

It was no good. I was surrounded,
trapped like an animal caught in the nets. I'd be fed
to the Minotaur, or to one of the heads
of the Hydra. By fighting I only made matters worse:
*seven* sentries appeared, where before was one nurse.

I climbed on the couches, knocked over a chair,
hid in an alcove to block out the glare
of a light. Cupid was nowhere. The voices of my sisters screamed,
'He's not your lover! He's a monster!' In a living dream
I'd become Odysseus in the Cyclops' cave,
about to be swallowed with no chance of being saved.

They said *No One* would hurt me, but I guessed their game:
I knew that *No One* was *Somebody*'s name.
They sharpened a needle for the eye of my mind,
speared it in, till I felt myself fade and go blind,
freefalling into a blackened abyss,
forever shut out from the day, like Oedipus.

Then I turned into Sisyphus pushing a rock,
as I struggled to keep awake, to swim back to the top.
Next I was Aeneas in Hades, the nurses were ghosts.
I was Psyche again when I awoke.

This room is silent now. On the door is a number
in washable ink. I wear a hospital toga.
When the nurse comes in with more drugs, she will say
in a mocking tone, 'How is Aeneas today?'
Yes, yesterday with racing thoughts and clenched fist,
I can say life was faster and fuller than this.

## Metamorphosis

I dreamt my illness turned my scalp to plastic,
that my brain became a walnut-shaped, white helmet,
through which my hair grew, so strangers knew my secret,
and when they saw me, crossed the street in panic,
as if I wore a T-shirt saying *Schizophrenic*,
and they didn't stop to think I take my tablets.

# Classical Illusion

Jack read Greek texts, like a wise old owl
depicted on an Athenian coin.
While wet Oxford winter winds would howl
round weathered spires, he would enjoin
himself not to tire of complex lines,
measuring out his life with epsilons,
iota subscripts, rough breathing signs,
dactyls, spondees and upsilons,
a priestly votary of Artemis,
ensconced in Aristotelian bliss.

Alice used to pass him in the College quad.
His black gown billowed in the evening breeze.
In The High, The Turl, or in the Bod.,
she used to glimpse him and be pleased.
He was fatherlike and a kind of god,
but as she drew near, she would feel unease.
He would never smile, he would never nod.
His self-sufficiency made her freeze.
The fondness she bore him was frenzied, odd,
dangerous as the sword of Damocles.

He taught her the patterns of ancient plays,
of Phaedra's excess and Medea's fall,
of Dido in Hades, who turned away,
of Aeneas, who followed duty's call.
She listened acutely to every phrase.
She kept looking out for his face in Hall.
She kept the image of his brown-eyed gaze.
As though by Furies, she had been enthralled.
Carthage was ruined and she was crazed,
too blind to see the writing on the wall.

She saw him last in a term Collection,
where the dons criticised her lack of drive.
She soon became lost in introspection,
till her sanity took a headlong dive.

Rejection pushed her over the precipice
into a world of imagined fear,
a living hell, where Jack played Dis
and she could visit for half the year.
Now Alice lies in a hospital bed,
alone with Hippolytus inside her head.

## Single Volume

They say he lives outside the real world,
sheltered in a College staircase room,
as winter settles into evening gloom,
contented as a cat whose tail's curled
and twitches now and then in satisfaction,
reading Aristotle's ancient words,
agreeing it is better to prefer
the life of study to the life of action.
Scholars come and go like long-lost summers,
young men who ridicule his careful style,
young girls who learn to love his nervous smile.
He translates the same old tale for every comer.
The radius of his sight is but one mile,
and the woman on the phone is just his mother.

# Flight

The mother blackbird I've been feeding
has flown in the open door of the kitchen,
where she flutters against the stuck window,
like a butterfly, finding no way through.

A startled eye stares. In the flap of a wing
it all comes back: my heart beating
so fast I thought it would explode,
my mind and body in overload,

running the corridors, fleeing nurses,
who seemed stranger than another species,
then trapped in a room with nowhere to go,
how I was cornered at a safety window,

which opened only far enough for air,
how I didn't know there was no cause to fear,
how they outnumbered me, fastened their grip,
laid me down and injected me, like rape.

I cup the bird gently in my hands, like water,
carry her out, as if a Section order
has been lifted, give her to the air,
then watch her spread her wings and soar.

# Digitalis

As a child I used to sift
through batches of grass
for four-leaf clovers.

Each three-headed stem
on the factory floor
looked the same as the others.

That summer a bee
must have cross-pollinated
a foxglove and hollyhock.

The freak flower stood tall,
despite being stuck
in nature's cul-de-sac.

Its petals opened wide,
a satellite dish
receiving strange radar,

ultrasonic waves,
the likes of which
most gardens can't hear.

I marvelled at it,
unaware I was growing
up schizophrenic,

neither better nor worse
than anybody else,
just different.

# Cosmic Confusion

The doctor's diagnosis of acute psychosis
suffices to explain the mechanics of the brain,
but fails to clarify the thoughts that overlie
neuronal misconnections, for medical corrections
work only at the synapse. But isn't there perhaps
a better explanation for cortex complication,
a theory like a dart, that pierces to the heart
and formulates a cure, whose remedies endure?

For mental scars are weals medication leaves unhealed,
deep-rooted wounds and marks, dormant as dying sparks,
which a single touch of flame can fan to fire again,
as when someone's words remind you how you heard
bizarre interpretations of normal conversations
and bring back memories of how it felt to see
friends and family as zombie enemies,
when insignificances were not coincidences,

but intelligible signs *They* left for you to find.
What is needed is a notion of what causes the commotion,
an answer that is fitter than a chemical transmitter
to attribute to the scene. A ghost in the machine?
Or spontaneous mutation, causing all the aggravation
at the level of the gene? Has there always been
a principle of chaos, stretching far across
the universe from omicron to the smallest positron,

particle unruliness, like Greek gods and goddesses,
fooling with the lives of us, some cruel and some propitious,
free and fundamental things, pulling at our puppet strings,
guiding action, thought and will, which we are unable still
to harness and control in any finite mould?
Is it due to such a whim of somesuch microscopic thing
that maggots can invade my thought, and I and others can be caught,
netted fishlike in the seas, beached off-course by chance disease?

## Calypso

Not only in my dreams have I visited an island,
carried far out to sea,
an Eden of extremes, where I dance naked on the sand
and laugh euphorically,

but also suffer storms, as threatening thunder reaches
nearer and still nearer,
a paradise of palms, which sees hell rain on its beaches
schizophrenic weather.

Here I have a sailcloth I filled with a shell, a pebble,
a ticket with a tear,
whose return half got lost, and a message in a bottle
to prove that I was there.

# Rhapsody in B Flat

You must play the Nazarene,
acting out that Calvary scene.
The tabernacle's torn asunder.
Cue the lightning and the thunder.
Change of backdrop. Lights. Stonehenge.
Hooded Druids seek revenge,
circling you with blazing torches,
held so close a bright flame scorches.

Far across the Indian sea,
robed in saris for suttee,
you can't hear as you scream out loud
above the clamour of the crowd.
Now they stoke your witch's pyre,
burning you in hellish fire.
Flames are leaping high and wild.
They're casting in your newborn child.

Next you're in a ducking chair
to see how well your powers fare.
Drown breathlessly and save your name,
or live and face the funeral flame.
Down a foggy city street
footsteps follow. You retreat,
hurry on wet cobbles, slip,
and the Ripper's got his grip.

Then in modern stereo
comes a tune that's deep and low,
as a jackal-headed mask
locks you in a mummy's cask.
Look out. Satan's army's coming.
Can you hear your heartbeat drumming?
Like a hunted fox that's running,
you're the sacrifice they're gunning.

Help's no use. They got there first
and with electric shocks reversed
the hearts of those you love and trust.
You know too much. You must be hushed.
Action stations. Red alert.
Save this human being from hurt.
Retaliate. Stand up and fight.
Or cut your losses. Christ, take flight.


## Benjamin

Benjamin was like a child,
gentle as a lamb.
Because he didn't think straight,
the vicar thought him damned,
the village boys threw stones at him,
the doctor diagnosed
him half-witted, and admitted him
to hospital, where on a whim
they administered a drug to him
and cut his temporal lobe.

A year has come and gone
since he sat with me by the stream.
The village folk don't even know
if Benjamin can dream.
All day long and all night too,
so some people say,
he sits still as a summer's breeze,
while physicians poke and squeeze
and work out their analyses,
and I quietly pray.

## Blues on the Tube

Ever thought of riding the rapids on the tube,
just for the hell of it, to keep yourself amused,
hopping on and off, going with the flow,
no place you've got to be, nowhere to go?
Ever tried to balance, to let go of the rail,
to stand up at stations and learn how to sail,
then jumped from the fish bowl and stared back in
at each gaping mouth and redundant limb?
Ever cruised the network just for the thrill?
*Mental Illness Need Not Mean You're Mentally Ill.*
Ever read that poster? Ever lost the thread,
or felt thoughts speeding up, like trains inside your head?
Ever tried to get back home, but felt too confused?
That's Circle Line jaundice, Piccadilly Line blues.


## Cerebral Thought

Sitting on a Gatwick flight,
I look at London, lit at night.
Orange streetlamps down below
glow like a brain scan done to show

axons, nuclei and dendrites.
In cells the size of meteorites
I'm just one impulse carried back
across a giant synaptic gap.

## Burial Goods

If I were going the great journey
and could pack my grave,
like a Neolithic burial,
I'd take with me:

a library of poetry
to remember the earth by,
a pen and paper
to satirise hell,

a sketch-pad and pencil
for doodles of heaven,
a direct line
to haunt the living,

the switchboard number
of the dead,
the Lord of Misrule's
extension at Head Office,

the ambrosia
of a billion Milkybars,
the nectar
of a never-ending coffee pot,

or failing all this,
a bottomless bottle of sleeping pills
to alleviate
the boredom of eternity.

# Word Tasting

First agitate the word in your glass,
swilling it round anti-clockwise
to let the air into the language.

Tilt the glass against the tablecloth.
Notice the colour. Is this word golden
or brick-red? Does the nose remind you

of freshly-mown grass or tropical fruit?
Is the word smoky or woody on the palate?
Do the syllables have a long aftertaste?

Has the word been aged? Do you like it?
Now try this. It is a controversial word,
the oldest vintage known to man. The seeds

can be used to grow this word in Europe
or the New World. Each climate gives
the word a different flavour. It's versatile,

easily turned into language. Growers love it
across the financial spectrum. Many find
this word smooth and buttery, fruity and ripe.

They say it is an alpha word, their favourite.
Some drink it early and often, others will
store it in their cellars for drinking later.

Then again, still others find the word bitter
and acidic, screwing up their faces, saying
it reminds them of cat's pee on gooseberry bushes.

There's no accounting for taste. Make up
your own mind. What does it remind you of?
In the beginning the label said *God*.

# In the Beginning

Empty darkness.
Uncertainty and fear
evoked their opposites.
The voices prepared to contend.
Their shouts broke the centuries
of stretched silence.

A chord struck sound,
fire split the night
and black burnt orange as sparks
plunged to burial in the shadows,
cooled to the dead elements
of a lifeless earth.

The flame quickened,
spun heated circles
until it reached
the limit,
and conquered by cold,
froze into the pale sun.

Still again.
Slow ice melted to water
and fear took refuge
in its dark depths,
hidden beneath a surface
reflecting the free sky.

Spirit uncontained,
the air descended
to graze the frosted earth
and life was born,
union of his sad song,
her echoes of retreat.

The voices balanced in its call,
two truths destined to oppose,
alone each worthless,
in conflict joint creators
of a world formed before man's mind
evolved its one all-powered God.

# If Nature

If I were other than I find I am,
not atoms with this body and this face,
but scattered particles, part of the land,
the sea, the air, having left no trace
of what I was before, or who, or why,
as I shall be when I am turned to dust,
then I'd not be afraid to sleep or die,
trusting that of all gods Nature knows best.
If she gives me to winds, flames, streams and mud,
my dreams will bear fruit, my ideas come to bud.

If Nature were my beneficiary,
and I bequeathed to her all that I knew,
all that I did and was, am and shall be,
then like a treasury, her revenue
would be gathered together on collection day.
As scales tip down, so her bowl would fill,
while mine was emptied. My last breath would pay
her back the debt I owe. I'd foot the bill.
The lease on life I signed in blood would cease.
My dwelling would be let to someone else.

If I were melted down, like liquid gold
from solid ingots, to be turned to coin,
or sown like seeds in the autumnal cold,
so that in warmer weather from my groin,
my breasts, my hands, my lips, sprang up the shoots
of plum, of pear, of apple and of peach,
from my heart an oak tree spread its roots,
and from my liver lilac branches reached,
then there'd be nothing left of me to doubt her.
I myself would become the answer.

# Driving through the Villages
*May 2001*


Posters have flowered in the fields overnight.
New names grow where the old ones stood.
I remember your campaigns, the sight
of our surname nailed in a roadside wood,
taped to streetlamps, staked in hedgerows,
suspended in overhanging trees,
displayed in drives and cottage windows
at every election since '83,
when I was still too young to vote
and politics was a photo call,
which meant I could wear your silk rosette
and be late for lessons one day at school,
find myself in the Bexhill paper,
holding up a raffle prize,
or seated on stage at the De La Warr theatre
before a sea of faces.
                             Most of them have died,
like the old lady whose hobby was racing,
who sped round Brands Hatch, or the old dear
who would smile at me, when you were speaking
in village halls. In the last few years
they've handed you order sheets at funerals,
like the last manifestos of your canvassers.
Driving home this evening, it seemed choral
voices sang, *The day thou gavest, Lord, is over.*

And I remember a service in nineteen ninety,
a little girl crying, the Prime Minister
quiet and shaken in the pew in front of me,
but most of all a young man's tears,
a face I knew from teenage games,
when I was Monty and he was Rommel,
now shattered by grief, exploding into pain,
as his car drew away over the gravel.

The bomb blew his dad's body into the hedge.
The by-election started the second he was dead.

# Eastbourne

Each summer brought them out again,
like gulls along the beach,
to gaze on the horizon
at a future out of reach,
or watch the pleasure boat board
from an *in memoriam* bench,
along with the holiday horde
and its salt'n'vinegar stench.

Winter would keep them in,
though on a brighter day
they'd drive out for a spin,
or have grandchildren to stay,
but this December afternoon
they sleep tight in their graves,
and Christmas lights are up so soon
beside the ceaseless waves.

# Full Moon with My Grandmother

Because your time is short, we draw it out,
like this early summer evening by the sea,
as we prolong our talk, delay the hour I leave,
though now the pier is lit with electric light,
or a winter midnight, when we stood and stared
at the full moon on the water, like a path
to the other side of life. I wanted to ask,
'Where will it take you? Will I see you there?'
The stars above are already burnt and gone
by the time we spy them, which goes to prove
a memory of dust and ashes lingers on,
and if we choose to, we may call this love.
As you sail alone to another shore, know
my footsteps in the sand are here. I follow.


# Cloths of Heaven

When I was a child, you sewed me dresses.
I unpack one, hold it up towards the light,
see its criss-cross smocking turn to kisses.
*I'd like it to be blue with butterflies.*

And so you found this fairytale print,
stitched puffed sleeves and hem with a loving hand,
as a surgeon stitched the place above your breast
to fit a pacemaker, where the skin is darned.

Today I wish you blue, as in a sky
where the future never ends, but lives forever,
and though you've no sight to see them, butterflies,
dancing like a barefoot girl in summer.

# The Close

Where do they live, the sounds of other people,
the boy who plays his trumpet out of key,
the woman talking at her kitchen table,
the snatch of a tennis match on TV,

the sprinkler on a lawn, set to stop and go,
the dog that barks whenever it is bored,
the music from a curtained upstairs window,
the wood pigeon which plays its stuck record?

Where do they live, in or outside you?
You ask till you no longer want to know,
because you can hear your own footsteps too,
and the silence of your shadow on the road.

# Judgement

What caught my eye was not the murderer,
nor the rope that swung, like a pendulum,
from the gallows, nor the guilty man's mother,
as she wept, as if at the Crucifixion,

and not the face of the dead girl's father,
haunted by reports of the attack,
nor the condemned executioner,
a black scarf tied around his neck,

but the trajectory of a gull in flight,
like a jury's verdict, starting to flutter
free of the courtyard, its wings white
as acquittal, above the pointing crowd's chatter.


# Time Travel

Were we to travel forwards in time,
would we witness the earth as it once was?
Journeying to the end of the line,
would we loop back to the dinosaurs,
the savannahs before the birth of man,
a sunrise no one could have watched,
continents linked as all one land,
days, weeks, months, no counting clocks?
Might we alight at the first heat,
when the deep brimmed over and flooded space,
when a gale tore through the firmament,
when a cell divided in the clay?
Were we to ride to the future's close,
would we see the childhood of the world?

# Shorts

### At the Birth

The first-time mother wouldn't settle,
had to be shepherded into the stable.
A farmhand put ropes round the calf's ankles.

Then with a human groan she stumbled,
and as the man pulled the bull calf slid
headfirst into the straw of its crib,

fresh as a garden pea from its pod.
She licked his chest to get his heart going.
I heard the first cuckoo call this morning.

### Gabriel

The centenarian tells how his grandmother
put wool in his granddad's hand in his coffin,
so when he arrived at the gates of heaven,
he would have on his person proof for St Peter
that seven days a week he'd done shepherd's work
and in the lambing season had to miss church.

### Atheist

She believed in the hymns she sang, aged five,
to her grandfather the night he died.
The god she lost was a white-haired man,
who never seemed to speak, nor listen,
to a small girl as she knelt down
by her bed, like Christopher Robin.

## Triptych

In the house of my grandmother
is a dressing-table, like an altar,
where there stands a triple mirror,

in which, as through a glass darkly,
I see a female trinity,
my grandmother, my mother and me,

before the vision turns to shadow,
a curtain flaps and through the window
fly three spirits: girl, wife, widow.


## Riddle

I am the action that's almost over.
I am the alpha at the end of omega.
I am the adult world. I am the joys
of childhood. I am atom and void,
two sides of a coin. I am hunter and prey,
black and white, wrong and right. I am night. I am day,
the road that will lead to Damascus and Rome,
the path to both future and past, the way home.


## The Mysteries Explained

A philosopher and a physicist
on a rock above the shore
prepared to offer the people the gist
of Ontological Law.
The crowd did not stir, arrived for their tryst
and the truth in store.

*We're forced to infer, as it were, we exist,*
*but we can't be sure.*
*The chance we occur is x over six*
*to the power of four.*
The cheated crowd hurled them to the sea's hiss
and the ocean's roar.

# Buridan's Ass

On Blackpool beach I was motivated
by carrots and sticks, easily sated
with sugar lumps from indulgent kids,
though I had my dreams. Of course I did,
wanted to bear the returned Messiah
into town, or find a big-time buyer
for a Cleopatra who bathed in pints.
Yes, *Aesop: The Movie* was in my sights.
Then I volunteered, bribed by extra cash,
for an egghead's experiment. That rash
impulse to grab the dosh and take the bait
was the last whim I had. I vacillate,
starving midway between two equal bales,
undecided as shoppers at the sales.
Now RSPCA photographers
snap me to warn of cruel philosophers.

# All in the Mind

When Descartes made up his maxim
that winter evening by the fire,
was he seduced by the ease of Latin
into making a simple truth seem harder?
*Cogito ergo sum*, he wrote,
like a magician casting a spell,
pulling from the black top hat of thought
the white rabbit that was his sense of self.
The subject hides in a Latin verb,
like a pearl inside an oyster shell.
When he found his mind's 'I' lurking there,
he believed he'd solved the Sphinx's riddle,
but it's plain to see thought requires a thinker,
as movies in brains demand spectators.

## Republic VII

I stare at the wall of the computer screen
so long, it seems I live in Plato's cave.
I notice words without knowing what they mean,
as if I watched the shadows puppets made

but couldn't link their shapes to actual things.
I sit like a captive, chained to a chair,
oblivious to the building's comings and goings,
but now, like a released prisoner,

I turn, blinking, towards the window
to see sudden sunlight, an April shower,
white blossom on a tree, somewhere a rainbow,
and fresh shoots bursting into flower.


## Chained Library

A thesis on liberty, chained to a shelf,
shoulder to shoulder with other books,
weighed down by the burden of knowing itself,
lost in the dust of anonymous stacks,
began to forget all the lines it had read,
visualised light and a hand appearing
to take it to the very edge of its ledge,
where it opened its pages and spread its wings.
Now its paper was white as a dove.
With each beat of its covers it metamorphosed
into the freedom it had always dreamt of.
It flew through the window because it chose.
A camera might have captured each printed verb
turning into action, book becoming bird.

# New England

No one believes until he is there
the reds of the leaves, the fiery flare
of yellows and golds. We cruised through the state
in the back of an Olds sometime late
in the burnt-out fall, for every mile
a pumpkin stall, or olden style
general store, selling maple candies,
settlers' lore and doodle dandies
from the Yankee war. We drove to the coast
and watched the shore with its easternmost
Atlantic waves, breaking in pairs,
whipped on like slaves, or white-maned mares.

Turning back to Cambridge, Mass.,
I paused to track a Harvard class.
I saw, as I scanned the Charles River,
my father as a young man stand and shiver
on a footbridge in the winter air,
under tutelage of an ivied square,
the rolling years frozen like painted lakes,
where muffled children on Christmas skates
play before whiteboard Protestant churches,
holly-wreathed doors and silver birches.

But there's one place that lingers on
unerased for me, Old Bennington,
where a grave on a hillside in plain Vermont
cradles baptised, as in a font,
the burnt remains of Robert Frost,
thoughts unexplained and poems lost
down below the ground another
year of snow will come and cover.

# In the National Palace Museum, Taiwan

Here in this entrepreneurial State
they work in night markets and evening school.
A Ming porcelain bowl shows Dragon Gate,
where a carp rises from a cobalt pool

to become that creature in mist above,
a symbol of strength, of the emperor,
of success – a concept these people love,
who fled from a communist conqueror.

In their port cargoes prepare to embark.
In their World Trade Centre the day's begun.
China Steel is the scale of a theme park.
Textile factory machines run and run.

But see how each busy capitalist
stares serenely through an exhibit's glass
to gaze at lotus flowers, a phoenix,
or philosophers on a mountain path.

# At Miletus

'Water is best,' Thales said.
He didn't have far to look for his answer.
Millennia have pushed the boat out,
coast and natural science moved along the road.
The remains are late, but a few stone walls

speak in fragments of times before his,
Minoan, Mycenaean, empires of maritime strength.
And did he stand here,
sand between sandalled toes,
feet on the shore, but head in the heavens,

dazzling in a tunic of brilliant white,
transfixed by the angle a sun's ray
made with a trireme out to sea,
a bronzed body going nowhere,
but a mind arriving at truth?

By tricks of time and place I hear
shouts of 'Eureka!'
as Archimedes steps naked from his tub,
then those of 'Thalassa!'
as the Ten Thousand glimpse the waves.

And suddenly thetas ascend,
like thought bubbles,
eddy into the ether to descend and pop,
condensing to molecules of $H_2O$
on an odyssey through the Aegean sea.

# Heraclitean Haiku

The water has gone
and the man who stepped in it
has also moved on.

*

Zeus hurled forks of light,
made heaven and diamonds,
Hades and graphite.

*

Winter, war, hunger
help us to appreciate
fullness, peace, summer.

*

Let me syllogise.
All things are fire. Fire is bright.
Thus all things are wise.


# On Samos

I'm swimming at right angles to the path of the sun.
Waves follow on like multiplication.

A guitar in a bar plays an octave higher.
There must be a note for each boat in the harbour.

Sails spread like a compass in geometry.
I could stay and count pebbles up to infinity.

The hillside is a hypotenuse.
The town's white houses have triangular roofs.

Pythagoras's statue stands on a plinth.
This is his birthplace, where numbers make sense.

# Statues

In the republic of dreams philosophers recline
with athletes, debating questions of body and mind.

Poets with laurels sit at the feet
of blind prophets, who shake wooden staffs at fate.

Orators in tunics address fickle crowds,
that hold the lives of armies in a show of hands.

Priests sell rumours to merchants and spies,
who sail home in triremes across wine-dark seas.

The gods lie about, fight, love, count gold,
while the first historians start to record.


# Prose Poem

The enemy, who had marched for two days with all haste from the shore, reached the plain, where their fathers had fought, but did not at first proceed towards the city, preferring to set up a tribute with stones, which they had brought with them for the purpose. Meanwhile, when it had been reported that the enemy were not far off, terror struck at the hearts of all those who had sought safety within the city walls. The assembly met and after a show of hands it was decided that delegates should be sent to the enemy in order that an agreement might be made. When after five days the delegates had not returned and the enemy had started to set fire to the farms, the citizens, by now very much afraid and with scarce supplies of food and water, began to pray in the temples and to sacrifice to the goddess in the market-place. At length, at dawn on the sixth day the enemy advanced and laid waste the city.

# Lesson, 1914

What form is the adjective in sentence one?
Well done, Jones. The *bravest* soldiers won.

Why did they go to war? Sentence two.
That's right. It was *necessary* to.

Look at the verb. Who fights in sentence three?
Yes, Watson. First person plural: *we*.

Now, which tense is used in sentence four?
Good. We *shall* be victorious in the war.

How many will have perished? Sentence five.
Excellent. *A great host* will have died.


# The Capital

I stood on the steps of the National Gallery,
which rose like a temple above Trafalgar Square,
and watched the drama unfold like a tragedy:

the circus of black cabs everywhere,
people and pigeons and handouts of bread.
I walked past the Cenotaph's fallen dead.

A bronze general in Whitehall was riding a horse.
Officials in Ministries were filling out forms.
Politicians' statues in Parliament Square

wore togas, declaiming debates to the air,
and Old Father Thames, like the Tiber, wove home
past the embers of empire of Britain and Rome.

# On Examination

You have THREE HOURS to complete this examination.
Spend five minutes reading the paper carefully.

If Time is a long-distance runner without a Start or Finish,
how long will it take him to get from A to B?

'In the beginning was the Word'. John 1.1.
What was before the beginning?

If the average man spends eight hours in bed,
how often is he having sex?

Time is lying in a coma on a life support machine.
Describe the shape of the graph on the screen.

If Time is constant, will the sun rise on Tuesday?

EITHER: Did December 31st occur in the pre-Cambrian era?
OR: Will January 1st happen after Armageddon?

If ten men work from nine to five,
how long do they spend procrastinating?

*Time is deaf.*
Discuss with reference to TWO of the following:
(a) Death Row, (b) the M25,
(c) Next Day Delivery, (d) our prayers.

Which will time an egg quicker:
a stopwatch, or a grandfather clock?

If we can put the clocks back, rewind the video,
and enter our second childhoods, could we ever revisit 1999?

Discuss the following with reference to Wittgenstein:
'Time flies.' 'We can't. Their path is too erratic.'

Old Father Time is your patient. What is your diagnosis?
(a) Alzheimer's, (b) live and kicking.

Three men have Cancer rising.
One has a short lifeline, one has bad dreams,
and the other has drawn the Hanged Man.
Tomorrow who will walk under a ladder?

*Monday, lundi, lunedi, Montag.*
Translate for the dinosaurs.

If Time equals Distance over Speed
and the Hare takes Concorde, will the Tortoise still win?

When you divide time, is the answer recurring?

Is history a circle, a wave, or a straight line?
(Illustrate with diagrams where appropriate.)

Which is longer: eternity, or infinity?

Now that you have spent five minutes
reading through the paper carefully,
write your candidate number on the coversheet,
but do NOT attempt to answer any questions.

# Agamemnon to Lear

If we could have our chance again,
if we could be rewritten,
make a comeback on the stage
of twenty-first-century Britain,
you as head of a software firm,
me as a drug baron,
this time we'd practise what we've learnt
of humility and compassion.

You'd star in a big-budget boardroom scene
in the chief executive's chair.
Your daughters arrive in a limousine
for the transfer of their shares.
The apple of your eye is only sixteen,
shy and reluctant to swear
how much her father means to her,
but just as your temper starts to flare
and you turn to disinherit her,
you stop and record it over.

As for me, I'm in a thriller,
about to make a deal,
surrounded by other bad guys,
who want proof the stuff's for real.
From the back seat of a black car
I fetch my little girl.
I'm sickened as the gangsters leer.
She looks so virginal.
Although I know it's murder,
I ignore her eyes' appeal,
but just as I give the drug to her,
I call *Cut* and rewind the reel.

## Socrates to Descartes

When on earth, you and I weren't sure of much,
only things, like God and Justice, one can't touch.
Concepts had to start with an upper case
before we would let them past second base.
But the old days were good: you by your fire,
glass in hand, me with ouzo and a lyre,
dancing girls on a Platonic table,
and young lads. Of what weren't we capable?

You see it's the physical stuff I miss.
Since the hemlock, I've put emphasis
on experience, not universals,
on live performance, not dress rehearsals.
In the heavens we spin through thought and space,
but want feet on the ground, a heart, a face.
Reduced to brains in a galactic vat,
we'd trade Ideas to get our bodies back.

# Young Man in Bronze

The young man slouches his weight on one leg,
propping up an imaginary bar which serves
retsina in pint glasses.
You get the feeling he spent last night
profaning the mysteries,
and mutilated some statues on the way home.

This is the artist at his most provocative.
He had a preference for this model,
used to vie to be the one
to anoint him with oils down at the club,
got badly into debt at some point,
because of the lad's appetite for horses.

He cast the features lovingly,
laid the victor's laurel on his head like a halo,
didn't miss a detail,
not a curl, not a muscle. You can see
youth's arrogance in the tilt of his face.
His whole body bursts with potential movement.

When Greece became a province,
he was flogged as booty to a dealer in Rome,
who sold him off to a senator.
He was given pride of place in the atrium,
alongside marble busts of the ancestors,
and was much admired by guests.

Today he stands in a museum,
daring tourists to avert their eyes,
like a pop star on his pedestal.
I run my fingers over his body,
but where there should be warmth
the bronze is cold.

## Modern Poet

I first heard him transmitted live
from a car boot sale this side of Hythe,
plugging signed copies of his books
among chipped saucers and fishing hooks,
on tour with his latest re-release,
*The Boy Who Only Wants to Please.*

He spoke in lilting, northern song,
like an anthem filling a stadium,
graffiti for Leeds or Newcastle,
a busker's tune in a shopping mall,
broadcasting living's shakes and knocks
like a twentieth-century *populi vox.*

I met him next as a pamphleteer
in the South Bank library, a pioneer
of colloquial, lyrical, metrical stuff,
a sibilant snake who had shed the slough
of an angry young man's metaphor
and abided now by Hampstead's law.

Then he caught my eye in the *TLS*,
reviewed by one as quite the best
spokesman for Generation X,
a cynical soul who is vicious, vexed.
Here, there, he scatters soundbite blues
on ageing, love, the state and booze.

So his fame goes on from strength to strength.
From the M6 flyover to the length
of the Sussex Downs he plays his tricks
to readers in need of another fix
of his bruiser's streetwise cracks and truths,
his workman's well-turned craft that soothes.

Look that's him, the one that's tipped
to be next in line for the Laureateship.
He's wiping the file that says *Eng. Lit.*,
the Byron, Keats and Wordsworth bit.
He's taking his place in the canon, our man,
and if Faber can't catch him, nobody can.

# Poets' Parliament

Suppose poets stood for Parliament,
that they ran as Independent candidates,
canvassing streets on council estates
with poems printed on cards which said,
'Sorry you were out when I called.'
Suppose they read in village halls
to one man and a dog. Suppose they formed a party
and romped home with a landslide victory,
that after the General Election,
their maiden speeches were their first collections.

Imagine they took their seats in the Chamber,
resting their feet on its benches' green leather,
whilst at the Despatch Box the Junior Minister
for Sonnets held forth on the merits of metre,
as 'Order! Word order!' was called by the Speaker.
Imagine the Gallery full of Strangers,
recognising bards from Panorama,
or interviews held on College Green
about their favourite poems for the News at Ten.
Imagine poets' statues in Parliament Square
to Pope and Cope, or Ted and Sylvia.

Picture poets pacing the Committee Corridor,
composing a line instead of toeing one,
or seated at tables in the Tea Room alone,
scribbling on envelopes which bear the portcullis.
Picture them sipping Pimms on the Terrace,
with memos in verse circulating in Ministries,
along with rhymed soundbites on Government policies.
Picture poets of the past, now in the canon,
kicked up to the Lords, like Elysium,
as if the dead had wandered over
from across the road in Poets' Corner
to sit in ermine robes, day-dreaming,
still able to influence a Second Reading.

And suppose that in Central Lobby the Saints
for England, Scotland, Ireland and Wales were replaced
with Dylan Thomas over one arch, above another Yeats,
over the third arch William Shakespeare,
and Burns above the last which leads to the bar.


## Here and There


When I'm walking in the city
past banks of offices and shop windows,
noticing the leaf-fall of litter,
as I'm swept along by a stream of feet,

I imagine I'm strolling in the country
past crowds of trees and parked hedgerows,
hearing the breeze change up a gear
and the river roar, like a main street.

# Geography

The earth was flat until I turned seven.
Due north was the deli at Notting Hill Gate.
South were the shops in High Street, Kensington.
The Round Pond was east and Holland Park west.

It was in July of seventy-six,
that long hot summer, a year of drought,
when we moved away from London's streets
and my horizons, like thirsty roots, spread out.

The world was no longer a level field.
North were the kilns of Ironbridge Gorge.
The Black Country furnaces were east,
the Welsh pits west, and south the blacksmith's forge.

Ragged Robin begged by the roadside,
Old Man's Beard slept under a hedge,
but what opened wide my innocent eyes
were the orphaned eggs, left on a ledge.

# No Man's Green

The only child I've carried is the one I've been,
who still asks where the streams and summers hurry,
or canters up the hill to No Man's Green
to gaze out at where the sky and fields marry.

You could stand beside the signpost, where three lanes meet,
and not know where in the universe you were,
straddling past, present and future states,
in Shropshire, Staffordshire and Worcestershire.

If you loosened the reins, she trotted back the way she came.
Left were the Sheepwalks. Once I ventured right,
rode on through a wood and the smell of silage from a farm,
and watched a storm of starlings, gathering for flight.

# Translations

I'm searching for a phrase to capture
sudden sunlight on a field of corn
and sheep beyond, grazing on a hillside,
like painted specks, the way the crop
shimmers like water and, overhead,
clouds scud across the sky like distant ships.

I want to denote this isn't any valley,
but the place I grew up in, that if I met a couple
ambling on the footpath, they would say hello
in a Midlands sing-song, that makes me feel
at ease. I'd like to convey the legends of the place,
tell of the house over there that is haunted,
the story of Charles II making his escape,
or the myth of a crowd linking hands
round the Wrekin.
                      If I were translating
for my friend in Brooklyn, I'd set the scene
in Central Park, with a curtain of skyscrapers
racing to the stars, and a backing track
of uptown New York, the city I was conceived in,
but have never visited. Or I'd rewind further
in her childhood, travelling along a red dust path,
that leads from a rice field to her father's village,
till I came to her mother softly speaking Mandarin.

How to render this in translation is a question
that goes beyond identity, nation, language,
memory, a love of the land, or the city.
The best I can manage is *coming home*.

# Word Hill

Not a hill built on words
torn from dictionaries, nor absurd
words with Latin stems,
nor Russian, nor Arabic, none of them.

Not a burial mound of archaisms,
of words with obsolete definitions,
nor a dig where archaeology
finds ostracisms on pottery.

Not a tip of Coke cans, baked bean tins,
train tickets, newsprint, magazines,
nor a land raise of verbal waste,
which villagers protest against.

Not a hillside tomb to Shakespeare's works,
nor stockpiled copies of a thesaurus.
Not the place where the gallows stand
on a blackboard in games of Hangman.

Not a bank of crossword clues,
one down, two across, none of those,
nor a stack of all the words
you could possibly have on a Scrabble board.

Not a hilltop fort, where tongues competed
and the losing language was translated,
nor the far-off peak where madmen go
to let their speech drift down like snow.

Only a Birmingham cul-de-sac,
like a needle hidden in a haystack,
where two girls freewheel down the street
sometime in nineteen seventy-eight

# Age of Awareness

Catkin days and hedgerow hours
fleet like shafts of chapel sun.
Childhood in a cobwebbed bower
guards a treasure chest of fun.

By the lake a fabled tower
vouches for a virgin nun.
In the vale a farmer glowers.
Smoke is rising from his gun.

Crimson and vermilion flowers
taint white beds of alyssum.
In the pail the milk turns sour.
Fairytales repeat the pun.

The defence declines to cower
when the time for truth has come.
The trick is sharing out the power
once the battleground is won.

# Magic

Happiness is a Midlands July
when I've just been nine or ten,
cantering on the Sheepwalks
when the lambs are fully grown,
before the wheatfields turn to stubble
and the blackberries have ripened.

It's an August afternoon
whiled in the kitchen garden,
eating damsons on the wall,
or polishing a bridle
on the step outside the tack room,
or scaling bales in the hayloft.

It's fading September light,
spent hopping between haystacks
on the last day of the holidays,
before I go away for term.
It's December back at home,
pheasant tracks on snow at dawn,

ice cracking in the trough,
church gravestones under moss.
It's the hammock setting sail
beneath the cherry tree in April.
Its digging with a fork,
the musty smell of baking earth

off seedlings in the greenhouse.
It's serving to an empty court,
a cornfield crying, 'Out',
a yellow dog fetching ball,
the scent of curry combs and manes,
hedgerow hacks, cowslip lanes,

ears pricked in welcome over doors.
Or it's the time Magic got loose,
and I stood beside her as she reared,
calming her fear, 'There, girl, there',
shepherding her back towards the field.
Happiness, that trust I mean.

# Pond Dipping

Children stand in line, as if at prayer,
being told how to dip their nets, once, then twice,
into water, pregnant with nymph dragonflies
and pond skaters. My eyes search their faces for

the son I don't yet have. The lake overflows
with life. Small hands empty trawled nets into trays,
take each catch prisoner in a glass jar for a day,
freshwater shrimps, a water boatman, a hog louse,

before setting them free, back in their element,
like old lovers. Now the excited shrieks
and baby blond heads are gone. The nets lean against
the wooden rail, like wombs, draining absence.

# Solitaire

Heard the one about the only child
who was the only niece and the only
grandchild on both sides of the family?
She grew up surrounded by a forest of adults,
the fairy doll on top of the tree.
Her parents told her they loved no other.

There was no sister to pull her hair,
no brother to fight, like the time she saw
her friend's older brother hitting his sister.
She made castles out of wooden bricks,
lined up her toys and made them sit
attentively before her blackboard,

pitted playing cards against each other,
evil armies of Clubs and Diamonds
battling white knight Hearts and Spades,
hunted with her dog through fields and streams,
rode her pony as if she were a highwayman,
and wrote poems to solitude in peace. Slowly

she became aware of an evolutionary bottleneck,
as if she were the only one alive on the planet,
the last person left in the empty room
to *turn off the light before you leave*,
the final stone on top of the pyramid.
One day she would have to launch off

into space and found her own people.
And now more and more she dwells
on her great-grandmother, herself an only child,
the way the grand piano went, and the money
gradually dwindled with seven children,
like her reserves of patience as her days

filled with noise, or the love she had stored
in her heart's cellar, parcelled out like war rations,
equally shared, and how at the end of her years,
she would sit by the fire at Christmas,
silent in the midst of a sea of voices,
smiling at the world she had created.

# Sisterhood

It began with a broad bean in a jar,
sending out shoots on pink blotting paper,
sprouted like sticky buds in Cheltenham streets,
witnessed a flasher on the way to Field,

spread like the rumour of our form teacher
holding hands with a young Latin master,
or the girl who spent half term on a boat
with her boyfriend, instead of going home.

It rose like sap, or the Nile flood,
appeared in French on a skirt, stained with blood,
bloomed beneath aertex shirts and sweaters,
showed off its legs in short summer dresses.

Prefects paraded it down the Prom,
wearing schoolboys, like badges, on each arm.
It grew like names on scholarship boards,
broke the silence rule, ran in corridors,

taught us to be writers, doctors, chairmen,
and showed in the manner we carried our burdens,
those booksacks we hoisted on hips, the way women
in Africa instinctively balance their children.

# Joint School Dance

We had red lipsticks,
rationed beer
and wounded pride,

dancing to victory
with shipped-in troops,
like G.I. brides.


# Latin Love

*amo, amas, amat.*
I learnt it all by heart
in cloistered classrooms, sat
whilst Cupid shot his dart.

Though Passive and Imperfect,
I mastered every Noun
to please Venus's Object
in his flowing, toga'd gown.

Stoically I bore it,
the Negation of my love,
for I was Subordinate,
but when I turned pedagogue

and saw a pupil's glance
look Conditional at mine,
I knew there was a chance,
though neither Place, nor Time.

# Variations on a Theme

### One-night stand

The vulnerable side of yourself
was voiced by the poets on your shelf.

### Nightlife

We must have stood out like a sore thumb,
four English tourists at 2 a.m.,
sampling Hairoun beer and the local scene
at an outdoor rave in the Grenadines.
I was sure the two teenage sisters
I'd travelled with would get the offers,
but the Caribbean men preferred
my fuller, more West Indian curves,
and as I was groped by the doped and pissed,
it was not their brother, a Wykehamist,
but Blacker, a Rasta, who raised his hand,
'Dat no way ta treat a woman, man.'

# Hubris

I am a white man.
It is my goal to bring
my gods, my laws, my fighting
into your country, to penetrate upstream
as far as I can.
I have a dream.

I have a dream
to expand my mill,
to found a hospital for the ill.
My workers' health will benefit.
I have a scheme
and I shall profit.

And I shall profit
from the Judgement of Christ.
For I am good. I proselytise.
I speak in tongues to convert the heathen.
If I talk enough of it,
I shall go to heaven.

I shall go to heaven
with *you*, my dear.
With your big, blue eyes and your long, blonde hair
I can be sure that you will breed
a race of men
to carry on my greed.

# Underground

As I stepped from the lift in Hampstead Tube,
I sensed I was walking among the dead.
The ghost of a woman floated past,
as a gust from the tunnel touched my neck.
The board said the next train was due in a minute
and was bound all the way for purgatory,
but if you wanted to go to hell,
you'd have to wait another three.
Posters were selling a pension plan
to secure the future for eternity,
and package holidays to heaven
in unspoilt Highland scenery.

The train for purgatory didn't stop.
Driverless, it sped through silently
with all its lights out. Shadows stood packed
in carriages, like coffins' bodies.
The next train said HADES on the front
in a light that might have been from candles.
It flickered and shuddered, opening up
its doors, as if they led to a secret passage.
A young man's ghost was playing a guitar,
passing round his cap for change,
singing how he left his lover
on his deathbed, as she held his hand.

A well-dressed woman had bags at her feet,
filled with half-price, designer shrouds.
A mother held her stillborn son on her lap,
comforting him as he wailed out loud.
A man in a suit read the morning paper.
The headline warned of long delays,
due to strike action and a shortage of labour,
for those who wished to be born again.
When at last the train jolted to a halt,
I stepped off to find I was back where I started,
took the elevator up to Hampstead High Street
and watched life go by with a *caffe latte*.

# How To Be Bad

Evil is the toss of a coin,
walking down the street,
the decision not to give

your small change
to the man in a blanket,
playing 'Yesterday' on a flute,

to go instead into Coffee Republic
and sip a tall mocha and Apollinaire,
in the gap between leaving the office

and taking the tube home
to your wife and new baby,
to drop into a bar,

when choosing a career,
being content to leave
patients and parishioners

to other people,
knowing there will always be
firemen and factory workers

there when you need them,
opening the papers,
to throw away charity envelopes

and the news section,
sure that someone else
will govern the country,

or be generous,
and standing on the boardwalk,
seeing a boy who is drowning,

to turn your back
and watch the fire slip
beneath the horizon.

# Rain

Look through the lens of this raindrop,
suspended from a pine needle,
growing fat and ready to fall,
like an expanding universe
before the big crash,

and you will see in its crystal ball
the world turned upside down,
great firs shrunk to stalactites,
and below them a sea of sky.
Think how old the roots of this tree are.

Hazard a guess at the ratio
of clear globes to needles, each tree
a galaxy of planets. And say now, Father,
are we humans caught in forest rain,
or giants pacing the firmament?


# The Architecture of Trees

This grand silver fir is a cathedral pillar.
Observe the fan vaulting of its branches.

These pines belong in the Parthenon.
Each one is an Ionic column.

Note the skylights in this forest roof.
Sun streams through each stained glass leaf.

This sitka spruce is a giant tent.
The dry ground beneath is a stone circle.

Each Leyland cypress is a highrise block.
Their towers are skyscrapers for birds.

# After Blake

And will chainsaws in modern times
roar among England's forests green?
And will estates of Wimpey Homes
rise up where England's woods were seen?
And will Coke and McDonald's signs
colonise these clouded hills?
And will they lay a motorway
among these outlets and landfills?

Bring me my Nokia mobile phone,
my Rolex and my Amex card.
Bring my grey suit. O roads unfold!
Bring me my S-type Jaguar.
I will not cease from working late,
nor shall my mouse sleep in my hand,
till we have built suburbia
in England's green and pleasant land.

## Fun with Donne

I could be your 'mandrake root'.
I'd like to see you often.
Though 'but Mummy', I'd look cute
inside a Y-shaped coffin.
I'm the mortar, you're the pestle.
You're the captain, I'm the vessel.
O Donne,
the fun
I'll have with you before I'm done!

You are East and I am West,
two points of the same compass.
Take off your doublet and your vest!
Let's go and make a rumpus!
I'll bare my body to your soul.
Two hemispheres can make a whole.
Old chap,
unwrap
the map that's landed on your lap!

If you look into my eyes,
you'll see your own reflection.
Have faith and your Sun will rise!
I'll aid your Resurrection.
Make gold with me, my alchemist!
Forget the sermon! Let's get pissed!
I'm keen,
fifteen
and partial to a randy Dean.

# Set Pieces

## *Nocturne*

Dug deep in dark despair at dead of night,
depression holds me prisoner from sleep.
That my fond arms lie empty is not right.
I, unrequited, cannot help but weep,
relinquishing the dreams that will not be,
the sweet, flirtatious glances and the kiss,
which I had hoped one day you'd give to me,
the sense of your first touch that I shall miss.
But as I cry, your features all appear
before my eyes. My mind fills with your voice.
I hear you whisper softly in my ear.
My heart beats breathlessly. It has no choice.
Although you are so far and unaware,
it seems you are beside me and you care.

## *The Ring*

It seemed as we fell asleep on the bed,
our bodies, facing inwards, formed a ring,
at whose core the earth on its axle sped.
About us the crystal spheres were spinning,
and even the sun revolved around us.
What kept our universe in constant motion
was an atmosphere of infinite trust
and the Word we knew, but left unspoken.
Although Copernicus has proved this wrong,
and we both exist on a distant star,
one of many satellites of a sun
that's going nowhere in particular,
it felt as if God the Craftsman above
had set us at the heart of a work of love.

# Prelude

I had a dream when I was young.
A cavalier with ringlets, curled
in black, and sash across him, slung
as on some beautiful Miss World,
whom Paris judges best, except
the real antithesis of girl,
reeking of cannon-fire and sweat,
would seize me in a giddy whirl.
There never was a Second Act.
In innocence I never asked
if after Marston he'd come back.
Between our lips no kissing passed.
By dark eyes I was never bored
and not once did he draw his sword.


# Overture

As a strain of notes on a violin,
played by a figure at a balcony window
in light which is fading to late afternoon,
floats down to a stranger in the square below,

and into the fountain of his thought
a coin is cast, or perhaps a pebble
is thrown in his mind's still pool of quiet,
generating awakening ripples,

so your eyes, holding mine for a semibreve,
seem each time like music heard anew,
and disturb my surface, like a gentle wave,
as the key of my gaze is tuned to you.

# Monument

In the temple I am having built for you
they are putting the finishing touches to the frescoes.
Michelangelo lays down his brush,
scratches his head, steps back in overalls
to admire the folds of your tunic,
and paints in your limbs with an appreciative eye.

Some are taking the wraps off a gold statue,
which depicts you reclining, larger than life,
while others nail a notice outside the gates
in an Oriental language, which translates:
*All who would enter must first remove their shoes.*
Incense on the air clings like sweat to a sheet.

At the far end Vestal virgins unpack trunks,
put dolls on beds in their dorm, pin up sketches
of you as Bacchus, try on white summer dresses
for size, stitch up the hems so they ride high,
belt the waists, go naked underneath, and slip-slide
past whistling workmen on the polished floor.

Outside on wooden scaffolding Pheidias
sculpts a shoulder muscle, strokes a hand across
the clean-shaven marble of your cheek, choosing
Aegean blue for the colour of your eyes,
hesitating for a moment, satisfied
with the image his mind is downloading.

Up a ladder a stonemason is carving
an angel on a pillar who bears your face.
In the gallery the echoes have been told
they are allowed to whisper only your name.
On the altar a figure in boxer shorts
is bound to a bronze cross, as if to a bed.

A frieze around the walls tells your life story.
As yet it is only half-complete, but see
how I've had them pencil me into the frames,
that haven't been filled. Though this tomb lies empty,
notice the likeness of the lord and lady,
with the lion at their feet, to you and me.

# Cross-country

Waiting for you under the clock at Euston,
a bag's leather straps in my hands have become
a horse's reins. I canter back to childhood.
The crowd of commuters are trees in a wood.
I'm jumping logs, ducking overhead branches,
as a voice on the loudspeaker announces,
*The 18:58 train to Manchester*
*is now at Platform 5*, and the concourse clears
to an open cornfield, where I kick you on,
lean in, sense your keenness, feel my thighs tighten
round you in the saddle, and inhale your sweat,
as you say my name, touch the back of my neck,
then pull me away, till I can't tell for certain
which one is the rider and which the ridden.


# Upper Palaeolithic

It might be thirty thousand years ago,
with horses and bison running the plains,
and you in skins with a bow and arrow,
holding me close against the cold night wind,

above us a sky, pitch black as a cave,
stars at intervals like blazing torches,
and our modern selves, descendants we made,
like two rivers, traced back to their sources,

instead of the twenty-first century
with late-night traffic and the cafés closed,
shop lights masking the stars, as you kiss me
on buried earth in Tottenham Court Road.

# On Southwold Pier

And I shall remember this, the way you stand
at the end of the pier, a figure against the ocean,
waiting for lines to wash in with the tide,
as the light fails and a man says 'We're closing'.
Thrown coins balance precariously on pillars,
offerings to Neptune made by those before us,
as we may fill a wishing well with prayers,
and find in answer mists, blowing in our faces.
When we set out, the sky was lilac and pink,
white waves were chasing wavelets to the shore,
arcing like dolphins. We paused to think,
fell silent by the sea's momentous roar.
I intoned names of beach huts we were passing,
Spunyarns, Sandpiper, Shalom, Summer's Lease,
each bright den shut away this October evening,
Lady Nelson, The Dragon's Lair, Icarus.
Waves breathed in and out, like a child sleeping.
Geese flew in formation, low above the water.
The pier on stilts was a flock of herons wading.
In the distance Sizewell slumbered like a monster.
Copper plaques along the pier recall 'The fallen',
'My favourite Sunday walk to watch the steamer',
'A much loved wife', 'The birth of my grandson',
or how 'We flew our kite and lost it here'.
I read their sepia memories and add my own,
a picture of you standing by the railing,
etched against the sea and sky in charcoal,
with the lighthouse eye, like a spy winking.
Winds that strike us are the poems we're writing.
I note orange lamplight ghost across my page,
look back to shore, riding the waves like Triton,
and see six gulls fly north, as we turn to leave.
To be still, together, before the sea's motion,
each in our own monologue, is a sign
we'll last, till we are swallowed by the ocean,
ship and figurehead drowned in waves of time.

## Pastoral

When I hear the cadence of your voice,
its songlike tone, its pitch and word choice,
something in me wants to fly the nest,
to build a bower from shining objects,

gather twigs and snails, feed open mouths,
the instinct which makes geese fly south,
makes us wait for spring to follow winter,
brings us briefly, or lifelong, together

to balance on a bough, and makes me sing
this solitary descant I'm now writing
for no other reason than its harmony,
like the symmetry of wings, wind in leaves.


## Fairytale

If we are all imprisoned by a text
we heard once upon a time, before forgetting,
and our lives unfold like the pages of a book,
as some play Paris stealing Helen,
while others are Odysseus travelling home,
and some dream they're Cain killing Abel,
and Romeo and Juliet seek each other out,
whilst every Faust makes a pact with the devil,
then I've come to see the story of my days
not as Beauty and the Beast or Cinderella,
but a modern tale of The Little Mermaid,
who watched as her prince married another,
except that in this version you are awake,
as I cradle your head above the waves of the storm.
You can see it's me who saved you from the wreck.
On the shore we give ourselves to the foam.
You win your tail at the water's edge
and draw the curtains around our seabed.

# Jewish Wedding

*(for Rebecca Ellis)*


If fate will bring you good,
this is a better way to court her,
in the garden of your childhood,
not stuck in church in the height of summer,
not with solemn hymns,
but with songs and dancing,
and dancers circling,
with a glass breaking, an exchange of rings
under a white canopy,
with violets and lilies at the start of spring.


# Newenden at New Year


Walking back from the pub,
I thought of the village church,
the altar beneath the arch
by which we talked and stood,

and on the humpbacked bridge
over the frozen Rother
I wondered how our passage
might have been another,

asking the dusk as we hurried
through the frosted field
if we were a century married
and buried in the Weald,

when wraiths on the steam railway
waved from the platform's edge
and a horse and gig rattled by
on its way from the farm to church.

# Villanelle

I'm driving down the alleyway of vines.
The tractor is a tortoise in first gear.
Then it's back across the fields with the bines.

At the machine the farmer's brother signs
to drop the load for hooking. Off I steer.
I'm driving down the alleyway of vines.

Two gypsies go before me cutting lines.
From the 'crow's nest' one drops hops on the rear.
Then it's back across the fields with the bines.

Above the final belt a woman mimes
chatter that her co-worker cannot hear.
I'm driving down the alleyway of vines.

By now I've lost count of how many times
I've shuttled back and forth from there to here.
Then it's back across the fields with the bines.

Tonight I shall recall how this sun shines,
still smell these hops and dream of pints of beer.
I'm driving down the alleyway of vines.
Then it's back across the fields with the bines.

# Toast

And though we can't predict, I liken us
to pints of ale, to firkins, casks and barrels,
stored in cellars to be shouldered up
and drunk by open fires in the winter.
And if I could compare us to a hop,
I'd choose for us to be the Kentish Fuggle,

which fights off downy mildew
and creates the right degree of bitter.
I see us planted southerly or south west,
appearing through the ground in early spring,
our young bines trained with twiddling
round the string, till the farmhand

in the crow's nest came to cut them.
Together then, we'd start on our long journey
from the trailer to a pint glass by the fire.
The tractor would be our going-away car.
We'd honeymoon across two fields of grass,
shed our leaves and sail along the belt

and fall into a heap of hopeful dreams,
from which we'd be transported to the kiln.
Someone would take a scuppet to shovel us
around the oast and then, when we were dried
and cooled, we'd hit the hessian sack,
till we were added to malt and water

in the copper. There flames of passion
would raise our temperature
before we entered the fermenting vessel,
where live yeast would spark
a chemical reaction, enough to turn us
to September nectar, with a taste

and smell which hold the autumn light,
as if it were an insect found in amber.
And as the hop is added to preserve
the ale for drinking, let us also last.
Beneath garlands of dried hops, my friend,
stand at the bar, and lift your glass.

## To the Reader

The words I write become another world,
where I am both the poem and the maker,
the creator, who decides what light is called,
and the *logos*, which is uttered by the speaker,
and in this place virtual love is possible,
and for the best in a parallel universe,
and happens on a planet the size of a pebble,
when you and I invisibly move the earth,
but this poem is only one of many
amid all the pages lost on library shelves,
and that planet revolves round an infinity
of other worlds and other people's selves,
and my pebble lies with millions on the beach,
where you might choose it, then skim it out to sea.